TAMING
YOUR
INNER
SUPERVISOR

BOOK TWO

DAY

TO

DAY

SUPERVISING

by Ruth Haag

illustrated by Bob Haag

cover art by Ellen Taylor

h·a·a·g

environmental
press

to Bob

you and me
side by side
hand in hand
always and forever

TABLE OF CONTENTS

PROLOG...IT'S YOU, NOT THEM

Everyone views the world and their place in it, in a slightly different way. Some seem very humble, some seem overly confident and some seem angry at much of the world, much of the time. When a person becomes a supervisor it is this view that they have of themselves and their place in the world which influences their initial actions. The supervisor's actions, in turn, cause their employees to behave in certain ways. When a supervisor is too humble, for instance, they might not be able to respond quickly enough to a problem. Knowing this, their employees will more frequently disobey orders. When a supervisor is too angry at the world, they yell at their employees too much. Knowing this their employees will ignore them. When a supervisor is too worried about losing their own job, they control their employees too much. Knowing this, their employees rebel, and refuse to do any work.

The First Step, Tame Your Personality

A supervisor is a leader who ideally needs to be firm, responsible, knowledgeable, decisive, and fair. This is very difficult to do if you happen to feel that the rest of the people in the world are better than you are, or if you are afraid that you will lose your job, or if you are angry much of the time. In order to become a really good supervisor, you will need to first be able to acknowledge what you are like, and then learn to tame those parts of your personality which conflict with your ability to supervise.

There are Three Different Supervisor Personalities

Supervisors and the views that they have of their place in the world are able to be lumped into three basic groups. The **sensitive supervisor** wants to avoid confronting employee problems and continually hopes that they will go away on their own. The **belligerent supervisor** wants to complain about every little problem as soon as they see it. The **regal supervisor** is so concerned about losing their own job that they want to keep control of every move their employees make.

Unless each type of supervisor learns to tame their basic inclinations, they are destined for difficulties in three predictable ways. The sensitive supervisor's employees begin to assign work to them. The belligerent supervisor's employees ignore them. The regal supervisor's employees eventually rebel and refuse to work.

The "taming" of these supervisors involves altering those habits which are causing problems with their employees. The sensitive supervisor needs to learn to confront people and even at times make people unhappy. The belligerent supervisor needs to stop, think and perhaps gather some data before they talk. The regal supervisor needs to put their own worries aside and concentrate on their employees by giving out information and responsibility to them at the rate which they need.

The Next Step, Changing Daily Actions

After a supervisor has learned how to tame their personality, they are ready to take the next step and   learn how to adapt their daily actions.   A supervisor will have to learn a new way to behave, a new way to communicate and will have a new responsibility to foster cooperation.

CHAPTER 1...A NEW WORLD

After Tenniel, in Lewis Carroll's "Through the Looking Glass"

A Story About a Meeting

Frank looked out over the audience. He was surprised and a little miffed. Out of a company of over 400 people, only 28 had chosen to attend this meeting. The meeting was held this same evening every year. It was such a tradition, that he had not really told many people of the time and date. He was sure that they knew about it already. This had always been an enjoyable gathering. He had an opportunity to address the entire company and then each of his department heads held an "open house" in their departments. This allowed the staff to see what was happening all over the company. After observing his small audience, Frank turned to look at the assembly of his department heads and found that about 10% of them were absent. He sighed, and thought "this never happened when Joann was in charge, that just goes to show how bad today's workers are". Since it was about 10 minutes after the starting time, he began the meeting:

"I am really disappointed that not many people came. This is your company, and you have to take part. I am actually pretty disgusted at your apathy. If any of you know why so many people didn't come, please tell me. I know I asked you about this two years ago, and some of you responded. To tell you the truth, I never looked at those responses. But, please tell me now."

The group listened to Frank's talk for another 20 minutes. Finally they were allowed to go to see the open departments. They had some trouble since none of the department offices were labeled, but finally most of them stumbled through the buildings and found most of the open rooms and displays. They were surprised to see one of the "missing" department heads in one of the offices. He said:

"No one told me where to go, so I've been waiting here."

They went into one department which had a large golf poster on the main door. Inside, in the departments head's office, were many golf items, along with a poster which said "Why work when you can golf?" This department head was a little irritable. He said:

"I just can't get my staff to work hard. If I even mention Saturday work, they rebel. I can't figure out how I got stuck with such uncooperative workers. I even had them help develop a mission statement for our department this year, and it made no difference in their attitude."

Another department head discussed his department's progress over the past year:

"We were working on a new product but the engineering department decided not to cooperate with us on it, so it hasn't been put into test yet. I get so irritated at Irving and his people."

In still another department, the department head was hard at work on her computer. She seem surprised and a little annoyed that there were people touring. She said to the visitors:

"Look around if you want, but don't touch anything."

Analysis: "Where You Lead, They Will Follow"

Frank figured that since the meeting was an annual affair, he did not have to tell anyone about it. When he was irritated with the response, he felt that lecturing to the people who did attend would in some way help make more people attend in the future. Frank also felt that things would improve if he asked for input, but then ignored it.

The group leader who had golfing posters in their office didn't realize that they were sending a very effective message that work was not as important as recreation. Likewise the department head who was grousing about Irving's department was showing that this was a company full of schisms, not cooperation.

Frank and his department heads were sending a thousand little messages to their employees, which taken together said "we are not concerned about you, and we do not respect you". The environment which Frank and his department heads created was not one which inspired employee dedication. However, when looked at realistically, employees were following the behavioral and verbal messages which were given. Frank made no effort to tell them about the meeting and they, likewise, made no effort to come. Frank should not have been so upset, his company was going exactly where he was pointing.

All supervisors want to have employees who are able to do good work. Many feel that the responsibility to do good work rests solely on the employees. Many supervisors become very frustrated with their employees. They make a predictable series of observations:

- These people are not as dedicated to working as I am, or as people used to be.
- These people never do the work the way that I want them to.
- These people do not treat me with the respect that I deserve.
- Some of these people are incompetent.

There are good employees and bad employees. The good employees generally were taught a good work ethic either in their home environment or at school. Bad employees are more concentrated on themselves, the perks of their job, and how they can get out of doing work.

There are good supervisors and bad supervisors. Most people's home and school years did not involve intensive training on the topics of leading groups and supervising people. Bad leaders feel that supervising is easy, and they lead without thinking about who their group is, or where they are going. Good leaders acknowledge that supervising is new, that they are not adequately prepared for it, that they will have to learn new things.

People who take up a sport with no training, soon find that they have bruises and broken bones. Likewise, people who begin supervising with no training, soon have groups of disloyal and malcontent employees.

A Thousand Little Messages

Each day, the actions of a supervisor send a thousand little messages to their employees which taken together say either, "I am a good supervisor, follow me", or   "I have no idea what I am doing, and I don't care about you". Employees perform well or poorly in response to these messages.

Behavior, Communication, and Cooperation

The job of a supervisor is to get work done through other people. To many supervisors it is a surprise that they will not be able to accomplish this unless they understand themselves and adapt their actions. Sending the correct thousand little messages each day is a skill which can be learned. Learning to be a good supervisor involves learning new behavior, new communication methods and new cooperation techniques.

CHAPTER 2...A NEW WAY TO BEHAVE: ACT LIKE A SUPERVISOR

A Story About Hank

Hank was a party man. He would arrive at a party early, drink a lot of beer, tell raucous jokes, and would sometimes literally be carried out of the room at the end of the evening. Hank became a supervisor. He was a good supervisor. He was concerned about his staff and their success. He had learned to "tame" his regal tendencies, and found that his staff respected him and thought of him as their leader.

Hank's company was having a Winter Solstice party. Hank knew that going to parties with his staff was helpful for their morale. He arrived early, as was his custom at parties, and sat at a table with his new staff members. Hank was happy to be going to a party. He had dressed carefully, he was wearing his tight leather pants and a muscle shirt. His staff was surprised to see him out of his normal suit. Hank enjoyed himself as he always did at parties. He told some jokes, drank 12 beers and laughed with his employees. Near the end of the party, Hank noticed a new female employee. He sloshed over to her and asked her to dance. Even though she was visibly embarrassed, he hugged her, and pulled her to the dance area. Finally she told him to leave her alone, and pulled herself away.   Hank went back to his employee's table, laughing. He said:

"She was a cold one! I think I'll try my luck with Meg next."

Hank's employees determined that it was time for Hank to leave the party. They insisted that they be permitted to drive him home. It took a while, but they were successful and he was safely put to bed.

The next week, Hank noticed that his staff members did not seem to be treating him with deference. In fact, they began to ask another supervisor for help, and ignored Hank. Hank heard some of the staff talking in the break room:

"What a jerk he was with Alice, and he looked so ridiculous in those leather pants, men over 40 should never wear leather pants."

"I wonder how his wife puts up with it. Did you hear that Ed had to put him to bed?"

Hank found it increasingly difficult to supervise his employees, especially Ed.

Analysis: Respect is Retained by Having a Professional Demeanor

As a supervisor, you have to behave as a "mature adult" whenever you are with your staff members. If you let your staff members see any actions or behavior which are able to be ridiculed, your staff will lose respect for you.

A Professional Demeanor is Maintained By:

- Wearing clothing that does not allow your employees to think of you in a sexual context.
- Keeping in control, and not behaving in any way which is repugnant to society.

Through your words, appearance and actions, you should send a thousand little messages which show your employees that you are a leader. You need to send these messages each and every time that you are with your employees.

CHAPTER 3...A NEW WAY TO BEHAVE: THEY'RE NOT YOUR PALS ANYMORE

A Story about Bernadette's Divorce

Bernadette had been married for two years. She was very unhappy with her husband. Work was slow, so she started to talk with her assistant about her problems. Eventually, she consumed the entire work day, every day, talking about her problems. Finally the day came when Bernadette decided to leave her husband. She enlisted the help of her assistant to help her move to her new home.

The inevitable divorce occurred, and Bernadette began to "play the field". Each new boyfriend was discussed with her assistant, and a detailed description of each encounter was given.

Bernadette's assistant began to come to work late. Often, he was absent from his desk. If Bernadette made a decision which he did not agree with, he simply ignored it. The entire staff began to ignore all of Bernadette's directions.

Analysis: You Cannot Share Your Personal Life With Your Staff

You cannot maintain the professional demeanor that is needed for you to be a good leader, if you enlist the help of your employees to solve your personal problems. If they become involved in your personal life, they will begin to think of you as an equal, or worse yet, as less capable than they are. They will lose respect for you as a person because of the perception that they will form that you are unable to handle your private life, and then lose respect for you as a supervisor. Keep your family problems at home.

Things NOT to Discuss With Your Employees About You

You spend a great deal of your time at work. It is only natural to share parts of your personal life with the people there. As a supervisor, you will have to apply some restrictions to what you discuss with your staff. Avoid discussing:

- Details about your personal love relationships.
- Details of problems with your spouse or children.
- Facts about your sexual orientation.
- Details about your social engagements outside of work.

Things NOT to Discuss With Your Employees About Your Employees

Often, the workplace is where people who are having problems at home look for help. While equal co-workers can enter into discussions of these sorts, it is best if the supervisor keeps distant from them. The supervisor cannot fairly and equally enforce rules to the entire staff if they are very involved in helping one of the staff members with a personal problem. The supervisor should avoid discussing employees':

- Details about their personal love relationships.
- Details about problems with their spouse or children.
- Facts about their sexual orientation.
- Details about their social engagements outside of work.

A Story About A Poker Game

Jacob liked his two new employees, Linda and Jack. He told them about the weekly poker game that he had with his buddies and explained that two of the buddies had recently moved away. He decided to invite Linda and Jack to the game. They all had a good evening and Jacob asked his two employees if they would like to come to the game every week. He thought that playing poker together would make Linda and Jack work more as a "team" with him. Jacob noticed that Linda began to slack off with her work. Jacob just could not bring himself to talk to Linda about the problem. He was worried that if he spoke to Linda about it, the poker game would not be so pleasant.

Jacob's supervisor, Clark, noticed the problem with Linda. He told Jacob that either Linda's performance had to improve, or she would be fired. Jacob decided to discuss this with Jack. Jack advised Jacob that Clark was unreasonable.

Jacob just could not bring himself to give Linda a real warning, after all it was poker night.

Two weeks later, Clark met with Jacob again, and insisted that he fire Linda. Jacob did. He told her:

"Clark wants me to fire you, so I will have to. I talked with Jack about it last week. I am sorry, but that is how it goes, I hope that you will still come to the poker game, we need you there."

Linda was enraged:

"If there was a problem with my work, why did you talk with Jack about it? You are unreasonable and unfair. How can you think that after treating me this way I would still want to come to the poker game?"

Citing the unreasonableness of Jacob's actions, Jack asked to be re-assigned to a different department. Now Jacob had no employees and no poker friends.

Analysis: It's Lonely at the Top

If you are buddies with your employees outside of work, you will be unable to function as their supervisor at work. Regular social functions cannot be shared with your employees. Supervisors need to either socialize with others at their same administrative level, or with people who do not work at their company.

A Story About A Solstice Party

Geoff had been working for the same company for 25 years. Geoff had advanced in his career and was now the CEO of the company. For the first 10 years he attended the company Summer Solstice Party. After that, the party got to be a bit boring and repetitive. The company had recently added five new junior scientists. The scientists were pretty excited about the Solstice Party. They arrived with their life-partners and looked around for Geoff, so that they could introduce their partners to him. They asked several people and finally were told:

"Oh, Geoff never comes to the party, I think he goes to his club."

The new scientists thought "I guess he does not think that we are very important, this must be the party for the lower class people." They were very disappointed.

Analysis: Business Socializing is Necessary

While you cannot become out-of-work buddies with your employees, some socializing is necessary.

Do Business Socializing, Such As:

- Company parties.
- Business luncheons.
- Weddings.
- Funerals.
- Occasional business dinners.

Don't Do Business Socializing, Such As:

- Weekly games like bowling, golf, softball, poker.
- Weekly meals where no business is discussed.
- Family parties.

CHAPTER 4...A NEW WAY TO BEHAVE: WHAT DO YOU NEED TO KNOW?

A Story About Knowing the Right Things

Sam respected his employees. He knew that they were human, and that they had varying needs. He knew, for instance, that Josh liked to have a big long to-do list to work with. Ed, on the other hand, got frightened with a long list, and had to have his assignments given out a day at a time. Both Ed and Josh were invaluable employees. Sally noticed that Sam's people seemed to always be very productive. She asked Sam how he did this. He replied that he knew personal things about them. Sally reminded Sam that he was supposed to keep personal life out of work.

Sam explained that while he took no part in his employee's personal lives, he did make an effort to know their work attitudes, and basic data about their home lives.

Sally said that she had asked her employees how they wanted to have their work assigned and that they had not answered her. She had even asked them if there was anything which would make it impossible for them to work overtime, and they had said no. Then they had not been able to work overtime. She repeated that she didn't feel that she should know anything about their home lives.

Analysis: It Is a Balance

While a supervisor should not become involved in their employee's personal lives, some understanding of what happens outside of work can be to used to adapt what happens during work. This understanding is rarely gained by simply asking the employee. It is best obtained by just listening to your employees talk. The easiest time to do this is during a meal. People talk in a more relaxed way during a meal. A monthly visit to the lunch room would be a good idea. You also might just listen to conversations at the start and ending of your meetings. Use the time that you are with your employees to learn about them and their work ethics.

Some finesse is required to keep a balance between avoiding a personal relationship with your employees, and gaining enough understanding of them and how they work to be able to create the atmosphere where they will succeed.

Analysis: You Should Know What the People That Your Employee Lives With Are Like

It is good at least to see and shake hands with your employee's home companions. Seeing them will help you to understand the stresses your employee feels. You might have an employee who balks at working late. After you meet their "significant other", you may see that they are a very demanding, rude person. Now, at least you will know why your employee balks. You, of course, will still make the requests, but you will understand the look of horror which passes over their face. Remember, this does not mean that you should get involved and suggest that the employee dump the "significant other". It only means that you will be more patient waiting for your employee to respond to your request.

Analysis: You Should Know Your Employee's Responsibilities

If you have to ask your employee to work overtime, it will be more successful if you know ahead of time whether they are single and lonely, or the other extreme, a single parent who has to get home to make dinner. For the single, lonely person, you might say "This project is going to need some overtime, can you stay tonight?" For the single parent you might say "Joe, I know that it is important for you to get home on time each day, but I am in a real bind with this project, is it possible for you to stay an hour longer?".

Analysis: You Should Know Your Employee's Basic Work Ethic

You need to know how your employee views working in general. If you ask "When you worked for Brutus Inc., Ben, did you work a lot of overtime?" and Ben responds "Yes, and that is why I quit, I hate working overtime", you know that Ben will have some difficulty when your company asks for mandatory overtime during the busy season. If, on the other hand, Ben responds, "Yes, we had overtime sometimes, I like it when the whole group works together to get out a rush product", you know that you will not have any problems with Ben's attitude, when extra work is needed.

Know basically what your employee's outside life and responsibilities are, and consider these when you assign work and ask for extra work. Don't become involved in this outside life, just be aware of it. Your employees will respond more positively.

CHAPTER 5...A NEW WAY TO BEHAVE: LEARNING FROM THE MISTAKES OF OTHERS

A Story About a "Bad" Supervisor

John was working hard to make sure that he and his staff were the best that they could be. They worked for their city's Chamber of Commerce. He trained his people to answer the telephones in a helpful, positive manner. Often he assisted groups of tourists in planning their visits to his city. He encouraged his department to purchase an answering machine so that visitors could be given basic information even when no staff members were present. His supervisor was very afraid of his own superiors. His supervisor went to meetings with the "upper management" with a fearful look in his eyes. John saw this, and thought to himself "Why doesn't he stand up for himself with these guys"? "Why doesn't he tell his side of the story and fight for what he wants?" John shook his head when he saw his supervisor go to his monthly meetings. One day, his supervisor returned to say that the "upper management" had suggested that each department should look into budget cuts. John agreed, budget cuts were a good idea, look for waste and remove it. Then his supervisor said that one place which "upper management" saw problems was with telephone bills. There were too many telephone lines. He said:

"John, I think we should remove your phone from your office."

John was incredulous:

"Remove my phone? Most of my job requires telephone work!"

Over the next several days, John fought and fought with his supervisor, and finally was able to keep his telephone.

Analysis: Remember "Bad" Supervisor Experiences

John can use this experience for years to come. Since he did not like what nearly happened to him, he can make sure that he never does the same things to his employees. He can make sure that his staff members get and are able to keep the tools which they need in order to do their jobs. He can also make sure that he acts as an advocate for his staff with his own superiors.

A Story About a "Good" Supervisor

Peter was the type of person who would be a belligerent supervisor, if he was promoted to that position. For now, he was a good employee, although headstrong. He worked hard at his job and generally performed very well. He had a major project due, but for many explainable reasons, he was going to miss his deadline. Once the deadline was missed, Peter's supervisor asked about it. Peter's supervisor was very angry, not so much with the missed deadline, as with the fact that he was not told about it, and did not have a chance to make any decisions himself regarding the product. Peter's supervisor called Peter into his office, as soon as he discovered the problem. Without yelling, or belittling Peter, his supervisor said:

> "Peter, while missing your deadline was not a good thing, what I am upset about is that you neglected to tell me. As your supervisor, I need to know when you are going to miss a deadline, ahead of time. Then I have the ability to find someone to help you, or the time to explain the

problem to the client. What is bad is if I find out about the problem because the client calls me to complain."

Analysis: Remember "Good" Supervisors

Just as John can think about the bad thing which happened to him, and resolve never to do that to anyone else, Peter can remember good and constructive ways in which he was told that he made a mistake. His supervisor took him into a private office, not in front of other staff members. His supervisor stated the problem and the solution, and the solution was actually logical and helpful. Peter can now model his future supervisory behavior after this good experience.

CHAPTER 6...A NEW WAY TO BEHAVE: PRACTICE WHAT YOU PREACH

A Story About Being Neat

Bob wanted his staff to always have a neat appearance. He chose a company uniform that would be complimentary to all body shapes. Bob also wanted his staff to leave their field sites neat. He visited the sites and personally cleaned them up, showing the crews what he wanted done. He ran training sessions covering the topic. Still, he was often discouraged when he visited a field site. Empty boxes would be laying around. Hoses would be run in a jumbled fashion, causing potential trip hazards. Time and again he would go over these problems with the crews. He made very nice speeches about "leaving things better than you found them". Still, he got very little improvement. One day it was suggested to Bob that he look around the company's main facilities and his personal office. He found empty boxes lying around. Extension cords ran from one place to another causing potential trip hazards. Files were lying about in no perceivable orderly fashion. Broken equipment seemed to fill every corner. "Could this be a problem?" he wondered.

Analysis: "Do as I Say, Not as I Do" Does Not Work

Many supervisors know how they want their employees to perform. They work very hard telling and showing their employees what is expected of them. They work so hard, that they do not have enough time to check to see if they, themselves, are following all of the rules.

When an employee sees you at work, they see you and the environment which you have created. They create their ideas of what is expected of them more from how they see you act than from what you say. The employees in the first story who had a supervisor who loved golf, got the impression that golf was more important to their supervisor than work. Bob's employees heard and saw Bob at the field sites, but also saw him in the company's main office. They determined that if Bob was too busy to take out empty boxes at the main office, then he would understand that they were too busy to do the same at the field sites.

If you want your employees to follow rules, you must make sure that you are following them also. If you cannot follow the rule, then do not make it. Make sure that the thousand little unspoken messages that you are giving to your employees are consistent.

CHAPTER 7...A NEW WAY TO COMMUNICATE: KEEP 'EM HAPPY

A Story About Making Dedicated Employees

Sylvia had a staff of ten people. She wanted her people to work hard and produce a higher percentage profit for the company than any other department. She read some employee motivation books and decided to try out some of the ideas. The first year Sylvia started a program called "the employee of the month". She chose an employee who did exceptional work that month and took them to lunch. In addition they were given a parking space close to the door of the building. By the end of the first year, each of Sylvia's employees had a nice plaque denoting the month they had won their "award". The company got into some hard times and Sylvia was forced to "let some people go". She decided to try to make it as easy as possible so she waited until the last minute, and then took two staff members into her office and told them the bad news. She personally assisted them in the final cleaning out of their offices.

The second year, Sylvia convinced the management to sponsor a trip for the department which made the largest profit. Sylvia and her staff worked toward their goal, but did not win the trip. There were rumors of a possible layoff at the end of the year, and Sylvia's staff began to watch her closely to try to decide if there would be bad news again. Sylvia went to meetings and came back and told them, "the corporate policies are of no concern to you, don't worry about them".

The third year, Sylvia began to get discouraged. Her staff was unable to make any higher profits and two of them had resigned after the last round of layoff rumors. She had not been allowed to hire anyone new, so her remaining staff was forced to do extra work. Sylvia was frustrated, she just could not get her staff to perform any better. They seemed to be angry and grumbled about their work most of the time. She went to the book store to look for another program. She wanted her staff to be happy workers.

Analysis: What Makes Workers Happy?

It just seems logical that a happy person is going to be able to work harder and better than an unhappy one. Therefore if you can create a work environment where the majority of the time, your employees are relatively content, you will have one where the majority of the time your employees are working hard. Some employers attempt to create a happy employee by giving them rewards and incentives, thus hoping to buy their employees happiness and loyalty. Can money buy happiness?

It is not unusual to read about a survey that comes to the "surprising conclusion" that money and material items do not make happy people. The "poor little rich person" is a common theme, as are the romantic stories that older married couples tell of when they started out "and didn't have anything". If money and material possessions do not make a person happy, then giving your employees gifts will not make them happy. What does make them happy?

Each of us can think to times in our lives that we were happy. There are some consistent themes:

- The happiest times are times when we feel in control of our own destiny.
- The happiest times are times when we feel a sense of belonging to a group and are secure about our place in it.

If you work hard to create a work environment where your employees are part of a cohesive group, and where they feel personal control over their jobs and their lives, you will have a very good chance of getting employees who are dedicated to you and who work hard.

A Story About a Rushed Supervisor

Steve called his supervisor and asked her for an appointment to review his report. His supervisor was hurried and rushed-sounding and said:

"I have something to take care of, I'll call you back."

Later Steve again called his supervisor and was told :

"I have a problem that I'm dealing with, I'll get back to you."

Steve tried to figure out what he had done wrong. Why was his supervisor avoiding him? What was the problem? Steve had seen Shirley go into the supervisor's office early in the day, was Shirley the problem? Steve asked John what he thought. He mentioned to John his suspicions about Shirley. John told Nancy that he was pretty sure that Shirley was going to be fired. John started to worry that he too would be fired, or maybe there would be a restructuring of the company? John went home and worried about it with his "significant other". They talked about John looking for a new job.

The next day the group came to work and discovered that their supervisor was out sick with the flu. The office manager said:

> "Did you see her yesterday? She was running to the bathroom every hour, I don't know why she didn't just go home."

Steve felt a litttle silly. He had been so sure that his supervisor was irritable because of the visit that Shirley had made to her office in the morning. He was pleased that he had only talked to John about it. Meanwhile, Mark in Purchasing was musing over what Shirley had done wrong (he heard that she was going to be fired).

Analysis: Make Sure That Your Employees Have Enough Information to Feel Secure

In order for your employees to have a sense of control over their jobs, they will need to be given the chance to understand everything that is happening in the company which relates to their job. If Steve's supervisor had said to Steve:

> "I am feeling very sick today, can we make an appointment for Wednesday?"

Then none of the gossip or worry would have had to happen. Employees are very ready to worry about their job security. You must make sure that you do nothing to feed this fear unrealistically.

Things which you should tell your employees about include:

- That you just fired someone.
- Why you fired them (just the facts).
- Briefly, why you cannot meet with them.
- That the company is in financial difficulties.
- That their job may be in jeopardy.
- That the company is doing well.
- That the whole staff is doing well.

It is easier if you tell all of your employees these things at one time, so that everyone hears the information "from the horse's mouth" rather than in a round-robin fashion. A regular status update can be briefly made at your weekly meetings.

Many supervisors feel that it is better to leave their employees "in the dark" than to warn them about upcoming bad news. While no one ever wants to hear bad news, your employees will feel more secure if you warn them ahead of time. This will allow them to make personal decisions in advance, rather than in response to a downturn in the company.

Analysis: Make Sure Your Employees Feel That They are Part of a Group

Along with feeling secure by having enough information to have control over their jobs, your employees need to feel like they belong to the group that they are in. You can promote this sense by:

- Having weekly meetings with them as a group, and discussing the group's work.
- Having them help one another, when getting a project done.
- Pitching in and doing some of the grunt work with them.
- Having some meals with them.

Summary

If your employees feel a sense of control over their jobs and a sense of belonging in the group that they work with, they will be happy. Material rewards do not replace these other needs. While you should compensate your employees equitably for the work that they do, do not confuse the value of salary and gifts with the need for a sense of security and control.

CHAPTER 8...A NEW WAY TO COMMUNICATE: ASSIGNING WORK

A Story About Ronda's Big Project

Ronda had a big project to assign. She called her staff together for a meeting. She began with confidence:

"We have been given a big, rush project. You don't need to know all of the details, because you wouldn't understand them. Rob, you are a licensed Professional Engineer (PE), so you will do the design. Marissa, you will coordinate the purchases, because you are the secretary. Henry, you don't have a PE license yet, so you will assist Rob. Now, here is a packet for each of you with your specific assignments. You need to get started today, and the entire project must be designed and constructed by June 1. Of course, if the deadline slips a little it is O.K. I always like to have a Plan B. If we miss the deadline, our Plan B will be to submit an outline of our work-in-progress. Marissa, you can start ordering the building materials today. Rob you should have Henry start on the conceptual diagrams today, and try to have them on my desk by the end of the day tomorrow."

As the project progressed, Ronda repeatedly asked Rob for the conceptual diagrams to be delivered to her, and finally, after five requests she got them, three weeks late. When she checked with Henry, he told her that he had provided the needed data to Rob, but as Henry said:

"You know Rob, he can never get paperwork completed on time. In fact, some reports which were due last year are still on his desk for his final approval."

There were many budget overruns, mostly because incorrect materials were ordered. When Ronda checked with Marissa, Marissa said:

"I ordered the same materials that we used last time, and when they arrived, Rob told me they were wrong, that I should not have ordered them until his conceptual diagrams were done."

The entire project was finally completed six months late. Ronda thought angrily, "My staff is full of such bad employees, why is it that I always have to finish up their work for them?"

Poor Rhonda, She Did Not Know How to Assign Work

Rhonda planned and executed her group's project in a manner which many supervisors use. She simply got her group together, handed out the project and assumed it would work. When it failed, she decided that her employees were just not able to work as well as she was, and that their stupidity was to blame for the project not getting done on time.

Analysis: The Assignment Needs to Involve Some Explanation of the "Big Picture"

Employees need to have some concept of where their part of the work fits with the others. If Marissa had understood more of what was being done, she would have pointed out that it would not be possible for her to order the materials before the design was done. Ronda, however, told her employees that they did not need to understand the entire project, implying that they were not smart enough. These sorts of comments make it hard for the group to band together and help the supervisor.

The "big picture" discussion, while necessary, need not be long and involved. Employees like to know their part of the job, it helps in making them feel in control of their work. The discussion should last fifteen minutes or less. Any more than this will result in detail overload. Your group will become bored and stop listening. You want them to see where the project is going, and what part they play in it. You want to give the thinkers in your group a chance to ask questions, and identify potential problems.

Analysis: The Assignment Needs to Fit the Person, Not the Resume

With this project, we can see that Rob, while a PE, is not a person who can get a project done, and delivered. Ronda needs to use Rob as a PE, but not as a supervisor or project coordinator. Ronda would argue that Rob is being paid a good salary, and his resume states that he is a professional, therefore he "should be able to do the work." The fact of the matter is that he cannot complete projects and deliver them on time, and Ronda will most likely not be able to change that. If she continues to assign Rob this part of the work, the projects will continue to be completed by her.

It is difficult for many supervisors to accept this concept. They feel that the resume and job description determine which person will receive which tasks. That concept only works when dealing with machines. People are variable. You will need to assign tasks to your employees and note how well or poorly they accomplish them. If their problem is one of needing more training, you will need to provide that. But in the end, some people are better idea people, some people are better deadline meeters, and some are better detail people. These traits are most easily dealt with by assigning the task to fit the personality. If Rhonda had put Henry in charge of the deliverables for the task, she would have had a better chance for success.

Analysis: If Possible, Allow the Employees to Assist in Setting Their Deadlines

Employees will feel more committed to a deadline, and more in charge of their lives, if they had some part in creating it. If you are given a deadline, you might tell that to your employees, and then ask them what intermediate deadlines they would like to set as a group.

Always make sure that your final deadline is at least 24 hours before the product has to be sent out or presented. This 24 hours will allow you time to solve unexpected problems.

Analysis: The Assignment Needs to be in both Verbal and Written Forms

Different people remember things in different ways. You need to provide your employees with a variety of detail-remembering systems. It is not enough to just stand in front of them and tell them details. You should make sure that they are taking notes, or that you have already made a written copy of the project on which they will add notes. Most people remember pretty well if they have written something down. Make sure that they do the writing, not you. You already know all about the assignment.

Analysis: Do not Allow a Plan for Failure

Ronda set her plan up for failure, in the form of a missed deadline, when she said "Of course if the deadline slips a little it is OK." People tend to make their work expand to fill the available time. When Rhonda told of her "Plan B" she gave one of the thousand little messages which said that missing the deadline would be acceptable.

A Story About Not Trying It Out First

Ruth had been supervising her planetarium demonstrators for over a year. On the whole, they were a group of people who seemed to not be able to overcome technical difficulties. If a light bulb burned out during a planetarium show, the average demonstrator would not think to change it, rather they would end the show early. Ruth planned for this and made sure that the light bulbs were changed on a schedule, before they burned out, and in her training she suggested ways to cope with this problem should it occur during a show. It seemed to Ruth that, all in all, she was managing to adapt her maintenance and supervisory systems so that the planetarium shows always ran well.

Lately, however, the demonstrators were complaining that the clock on the planetarium control console was impossible to read. With her tight budget, Ruth had not replaced the clock, but rather had attempted various ways to make it readable. Fluorescent paint and a red filter were her most recent attempts.

Considering that the demonstrators generally groused about the equipment, Ruth figured that the problem was not too bad. Then, Ruth had to do a planetarium show herself. She discovered within minutes that she was absolutely unable to read the clock on the console. Her watch was grey with a smoky grey glass over it, (so stylish at the time). Since the shows were extemporaneous, rather than taped, she was unable to know with any certainty when the show should be over.

Ruth purchased a new clock for the planetarium console that very day and vowed to check out what her staff was complaining about for herself, from then on, no matter how petty it seemed.

Analysis: Operate It Yourself

Make sure that any equipment which your employees are to use works. Operate it yourself. If they complain about something, go and look at it yourself.

A Story About Status Checking

Ralph knew that he should check up on his employees often, but he really did not want to disrupt the work that he was doing. He decided to call them one at a time and ask them how it was going. To his simple "Hi, how is it going?" he consistently heard "Fine thanks!". "There, status checked", Ralph thought. When his staff missed the deadline, he was angry, he said to them:

"I asked you how it was going and you said fine, why didn't you tell me about the problems?"

Analysis: You Cannot Do a Status Check on the Telephone

It never works to ask someone if everything is all right. We are programmed to say "its fine". You have to actually look at the work that they are doing, and talk about it together. If you are supervising someone remotely, have them fax you their work, or have them draw a picture of what they see and send that to you. If "one picture is worth one thousand words", then it would logically take one thousand words to describe a picture.   Look at the picture.

A Story About Criticizing Work

Ralph read a part of a supervisor training book which told him to check the actual work of the person. He was still pretty busy so he called Adam and asked him to deliver him a copy of the report he was working on. Adam spent the next four hours trying to finish up the report. He delivered it to Ralph at 5:00 PM when Ralph was leaving. Ralph instructed Adam to leave it on his desk. Early the next morning, Ralph looked over the report. He was angry that Adam had advanced it so far as to have drawn the conclusions without Ralph's input. He marked up the report with his red marker and left it on Adam's desk. Adam was mortified. He had worked so hard to please Ralph, and now this.

Analysis: Review the Project with Your Employee Present

You will not be very successful if you review the project at a time when your employee is not with you. About all that you will accomplish is to display your "supervisor personality". The belligerent supervisor will write aggressive notes all over the product and mortify the employee. The sensitive supervisor will just re-do the work. The regal supervisor will sigh and say to themselves "I won't be able to give them so much responsibility again."

Go to your employee and look to see what they are doing. They will not feel as threatened if you give them a chance to show you their work and describe to you what they are doing. Ask questions and listen to their answers.

Analysis: Be Careful Marking Up Other People's Work

While most people will tell you "I can take criticism", it is not true. People who say that only say it because they think that their product is perfect and you will find nothing to criticize. No one takes criticism well. Keep this in mind when you are reviewing an employee's work. Ask questions such as "Have you had any problems getting the old report loaded on the computer?" and "Is Sarah being a help with your research?" rather than "Is it done?" or "You have followed the guidelines, haven't you?". People are generally very aware of where their problems are, and feel much more secure if they are given an opportunity to tell you the problems, rather than having to defend themselves when you discover the problems. If you must write on a document and return it, at least do not use red pen. Find a color which is visible, but not too conflicting with the colors on the document.

A Story About Obstacles

Rhoda planned her next project better. She took her time before her staff meeting to plan out the work, and who would be best to do it. At the meeting, she gave a brief overview of the entire project and with the help of her staff, planned deadlines and intermediate deadlines. She then assigned the tasks. A week later she was checking on Bethany, her newest staff member. Bethany said:

> "I am a little worried about getting my part of the project done on time."

Rhonda felt a little angry and thought that her effort to plan the project well really had not worked. Bethany continued:

> "As you know, since I am a new engineer, I have not been issued a computer yet. I have to use Chuck's when he is not using it, and it turns out that he uses it most of the day."

Rhonda was incredulous. She did not know that the company did not issue computers to new engineers. She immediately went to the property office and asked about the policy. She was able to explain a valid need, and personally signed for the computer. She had a computer at Bethany's desk within an hour.

Analysis: Look For and Remove Obstacles Along the Way

Very often a supervisor is not aware of all of the policies of their own company. Most people pay little attention to rules which do not apply directly to them. At times a department head makes rules which help their department, and ignores the damage which will be done to others. Rhonda was not aware that the head of the company's property department had decided that new employees were at risk of leaving and stealing equipment, and so had made a policy that an employee would need to have worked six months with the company before they were issued a computer.

Bethany was sure Rhonda knew of this policy. Employees often assume that their supervisor knows everything that is going on.

In order to make sure that these problems are caught and dealt with quickly, the supervisor needs to be watching the task, checking for obstacles, and removing them for the employee as they come up.

Rhonda Checks and Finds a Mix-Up

Rhonda next walked by Henry's office and checked in on him. He was talking angrily into his telephone.

"I thought that I was in charge of that part. What does Marissa think she is doing, ordering the parts?"

Rhonda had assigned the new project in a much better way, but she had forgotten to remind everyone that they would be doing different tasks from before. Marissa assumed that she should go ahead and order the supplies just as she had done before, even if they had been wrong.

Analysis: Remember to State The Obvious

You need to make sure that everyone knows things that seem obvious to you. Make sure that you state the ground rules, every time you assign a project. Do they know:

- Who is in charge?
- Who is responsible to check the details?
- Will overtime be necessary?
- When should you be contacted with problems?

- What decisions do you want them to make?
- What decisions do you want to make yourself?

A Story About a Successful Project

Haag Environmental Company remediates hazardous wastes in soil and groundwater. One day, while investigating a site, a Haag field crew discovered a storage tank which contained PCBs. The Haag senior staff began immediate plans for the containment and removal of the PCB oil. This operation had to be done without a drop of the fluid coming in contact with the soil or a person. Even though the Haag personnel were well trained, the senior staff began to re-train the crew which would do the removal. First they had a meeting with the entire crew. With the aid of a marker board, they went over the planned procedure, step by step. The site supervisor took notes. Next they performed the procedure at their home facility. The crew dressed in their protective clothing and went through all of the steps. Last, they had another meeting, going over the safety issues and repeating the dire project consequences should a mistake occur. One of the crew adopted a cocky attitude stating that there would be no problem even if it did spill. He was removed from the crew.

Finally, the critical field day arrived. The crew got loaded up with their equipment and started off to the site. About two miles down the road, the van in which they were traveling broke down. They called back to the office and another van was sent, equipment was reloaded and the crew was once again on their way. At the site the crew performed the procedures flawlessly. The senior staff stayed in the main office through lunch, to make sure that they were available, in case a problem should occur.

There was no confusion, nothing spilled, no human contact occurred.

Analysis: Why Did This Project Work So Well?

What happened to make this work well? The supervisors set up the plan. They met with the entire crew who would do the work. They drew up the final plan with everyone there. Notes were taken. The supervisor and crew ran through the procedure together. The reviews were all performed well in advance of the actual project, so that problems could be discovered and taken care of. They removed anyone who was not serious enough to make the job go well and safely. The support staff was ready to help with problems, such as the van breakdown. The senior staff was available to help during the procedure.

A Sad Story About Bob's Seed Rye

Bob planned out his assignment. He wanted someone to mow the back field. He was developing a pasture and it was time for the first cutting of the Spring. He planned out his presentation. He took the person who would be doing the actual mowing and their supervisor with him. He showed them the field and said that one quarter of it should be mown this week. The tractor and mower were both working, he had checked that the day before.

The next day Bob went out to his field to view the completed project. To his dismay, a small swath of rye which he was growing had been mown down along with the pasture that he wanted cut. He had been very proud of this rye because it was going to provide him with his seed for next year.

Bob turned to Ruth and exclaimed:

"I did everything that you told me to do and it didn't work!."

Ruth looked over the situation and thought to herself, "Of course the employee mowed down the rye, it looks like it is part of the quarter field. How would he know not to?"

Analysis: Look For Failure Points

Mr. Murphy really stated in his "law" that you have to look for where things will go wrong and then design the plan around them. The supervisor has to look at their assignment and try to visualize where a mistake will be made. Sometimes its easy, if the mistake was made last time. Other times, some thought has to be applied to visualize what the employee will be interpreting from the instructions. It helps in a situation like this if the plan is actually drawn out on paper.

A Summary About Successful Assignments:

To have a successful project you must:

- Tell the "big picture".
- Assign the work to fit the person, not the resume.
- Give out the assignment to everyone at the same time.
- Write it down.
- Have deadlines which the group sets.
- Have your final deadline be at least 24 hours early.
- Have operated the equipment yourself.
- Review "side by side".
- Check the work briefly and frequently .

- Remove obstacles along the way.
- State the obvious.
- Look for failure points.

The Three Supervisors and Assignments

The sensitive supervisor generally can plan a project well, but will resist asking the staff to work longer hours, or at inconvenient times. The sensitive supervisor has no trouble reviewing the work of their employees, but does have a problem telling their employees what is wrong. Luckily, employees generally know where the problem areas are so a simple question like: "Where do you think there are problems with this?" will get the ball rolling.

The belligerent supervisor wants to assign the task and not think about it again, until it is due. They hate to do status checks. They want to make aggressive status checks saying, "Why isn't it done?" rather than "Have you had any problems?" They also want to short-cut the system by asking "Give me what you have now". This makes the staff run around making up a neat, time-consuming interim package. The belligerent supervisor needs to make sure that they go to where the employees are working, and look without talking. Then they need to ask helpful questions.

The regal supervisor will resist giving out the entire project. They want to make sure that they have total control over the employee. They also will resist allowing the employee to make any real decisions. The regal supervisor can try to avoid this by setting a goal of giving the employee enough instructions that they can work unaided for two days. They also can work on structuring decisions for the employee. For instance, they might say, "This part should cost no more than $100. If that is the case, go ahead and buy it. If not, come and see me."

CHAPTER 9...A NEW WAY TO COMMUNICATE: TRAINING

A Story About Herman's Lonely First Week of Work

Herman had been working as a civil engineer for a major public utility. He wanted to advance his career and so looked for and found a job with a government contractor, as a project manager. He arrived for his first day of work and received his ID badge. He was shown to his large office and it was explained to him where he could locate office supplies and additional furniture if he needed them. He sat down in his new chair at his new desk, beside his new telephone and awaited his work. Herman could have remained thus for a month or more before anyone came looking for him. However, after a week Herman finally left his private office and went to try to figure out who his supervisor was, and where they might be located.

Analysis: Orientation is Needed

Many companies have no orientation training program. They seem to think that people will pick up on what to do as they go along.

A clear, definite orientation to the company is perhaps the most valuable training which can be done for an employee. The orientation allows the person to learn where things are, what their work is, who their supervisor is, along with getting a look at the personality of the company as a whole.

Each employee goes out into the work world and represents the company. If the employee gets the immediate feeling that the

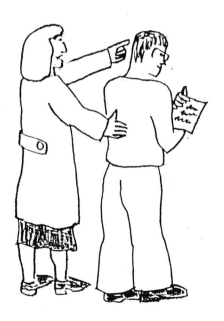

company is uncaring, or unorganized, they will begin telling the world that.

Orientation training is best if it is done by a person who understands the entire company, and can explain major policies and procedures.

Herman Begins to Work

Herman located his boss and was given an assignment. He had never done this type of work before, but figured he would give it a try. As he became confused he looked for other staff members to help him. Ed seemed most knowledgable, and gave Herman the most help. He handed in his first assignment, his supervisor looked at it and exploded:

> "This is just the same kind of poor quality work that Ed does! I thought you were smarter than that!"

Analysis: You Have To Train Your People Yourself

Herman's boss was a belligerent supervisor, to say the least, but what he was most upset about was that he had not trained Herman to do his job, and Herman had found and followed Ed's advice.

If you want your people to produce a product that you like, you will have to train them yourself. If you leave them on their own, they will be trained by your most outgoing staff members (and probably your worst performers).

Herman's Boss Trys Some Training

Herman's boss decided that Herman would need to be trained but he really did not perceive that he had much free time. He decided that Herman was pretty bright so he explained to Herman that all reports of the type Herman was working on were produced following a definite procedure. He explained the procedure to Herman, and the explanation took about 20 minutes. Then he told Herman to look in the file archives and find an old report to follow. He told Herman the job number for the report he should look for.

Herman took a bit of time finding the archive file room but he found it and looked at the job. It did not look like the same type of job, but he sat down to read through the files.

Luckily Herman's boss did know to check his employees often, so he strolled by the file room a few hours later and found Herman. When he looked at what Herman was reading, he realized that he had directed Herman to the wrong project. He sighed and sat down. Over the next hour he showed Herman the proper project and went over it with him.

Two days later, Herman arrived at his boss's office with a completed, correct report.

Analysis: Side-by-Side Training Is Critical to Success

Much as everyone wants to save time and have the new person fuddle around with assignments on their own, there is nothing to replace side-by-side training. If you sit down with the person, show them the task, then let them do it while you watch, they will learn in no time. If you describe the task in long detail and then leave them alone, they will almost never be able to complete the task.

A Story About a Training Class

Herman's boss began to think that training the entire staff in procedures would be a good idea. He called a staff training meeting for Friday at 4:00 P.M. He was pretty busy all week so he really did not have time to plan the training, but he decided that he could "wing it". The staff got into the room on time but the boss was a little late. He started the session:

"Um, I wanted to tell you what has been going wrong around here. You should always check with me before you start a project. I don't like it if you change the format for reports, and I think that we should re-organize the file room some."

He then droned on for an hour and a half. Many of the people fell asleep, the rest were agitated. As they left after the training, they were grumbling.

Analysis: Plan Your Training, or Lose Your Audience

If you are going to talk in front of a group, you need to think of it as a performance. You will need to know your topic and have a plan of the most important things to say. Also, you will need to monitor your audience. If they are getting bored, change your talk.

Key points for a good talk:

- Plan your talk.
- Think about your audience.
- Try out your talk before you give it to your audience.
- Make sure the equipment which you plan to use works.
- Do not read the talk.
- Have some interesting and, at times, humorous things to say.
- Be thorough but brief.
- Watch your audience and adapt to them.

Training should never be confused with disciplining. Disciplining is done in private. Training is "showing the way", not proclaiming mistakes.

Herman's Boss Continues Training

Herman's boss decided to try some more training. He was a little worried about the total cost of the training. He calculated that he would have to pay everyone for one hour of unproductive work. He decided to cut costs and only train the engineers. The computer technicians would not need to know the level of detail that the engineers would.

A few weeks later, Herman's boss received a notice from the computer support department stating that the "new" engineering program would be impossible to implement with the current software.

Analysis: It Costs Money and Takes Time to Train Your Staff

Many companies do not train their staff because of the high perceived cost. It is hard to put a dollar figure on the value of the training, but is easy to put a dollar figure on the hour spent in training.

Useful training which provides information that makes work go smoother is invaluable. Training just for the sake of it, or for only the "important" people, is useless.

Analysis: Everyone Whose Work Relates to the Topic Should Be in the Training Session TOGETHER

If engineers, technicians and clerks will all in some way be working on a project, make sure that they are trained together. When you train only the "important people", the other staff members become disgruntled and will actually stop providing assistance to the "important people".

Analysis: Make Sure That the Training is Worthwhile

Training which directly relates to the work that you do and the way that you do it is worthwhile. Training on the organization of the file room is worthwhile if your entire staff uses it. Customer service training is useless if your staff never speaks with your customers.

Do not be afraid to train on "sensitive topics". Every member of the staff can benefit from well done training on topics such as "equal rights in the workplace" or "religion in the workplace".

Do not go overboard. Some companies feel that if a little training is good, then a lot must be better. Training sessions should last no more than an hour at a time. More than that just gets boring. Likewise, taking your entire staff to a retreat for a week has very little relation and therefore, very little effect on how well they work together in the office.

How The Three Supervisors Do Training

Sensitive supervisors like to do training. This is probably because it creates a forum where they can tell many people at once how to do things, rather than facing one individual at a time. Sensitive supervisors can use training to tell the entire group how to do things, but must remember that if an individual is doing something wrong, they must be told privately.

Belligerent supervisors like to use the training to reprimand the staff for past problems. They need to keep focused on the goal of getting the message of how things should be done out, rather than the one of how they were not done.

Regal supervisor like to use the training forum to show their supervisory position. They must concentrate on making sure that their employees have the information which they need to be able to work independently.

CHAPTER 10...A NEW WAY TO COMMUNICATE: MEETINGS

A Story About A Weekly Meeting

Joshua had his weekly staff meetings on Mondays at 9 AM. He found that his staff was all in the office at that time each week. He began his meeting on time and first gave out general information.

"Next Monday is Labor Day and the office will be closed. This is one of the seven paid holidays for the year, if you want to work, you may."

Joshua paused here to allow the staff to finish chuckling. He continued:

"Joan is out this week, her son has the flu. She says that she will be working at home and anyone with any questions for her should be sure to call her there."

Next Joshua got down to specifics:

"I am now passing out our group's assignments for the week. You will see that we have a bit of work to do. Please look it over and contact me by 5:00 PM today if you think that you will have any problems with meeting the deadlines."

"Now I want to take some time to discuss the project which we all worked on last week. It did not go very well as many of you know. Kathy has agreed to describe what happened, then I want us to discuss solutions which will stop this from happening again."

After half an hour, Joshua concluded the meeting:

"Thanks for coming, remember to see me by 5:00 PM if you see a problem with meeting this week's deadline."

Analysis: Meeting Structure

Joshua has had a successful staff meeting. Successful meetings follow a basic pattern:

- The non-critical information comes first.
- The important information comes next.
- Important information is repeated.
- An occasional joke can be used, to have some fun.
- The meeting lasts an hour or less.

When your meeting starts, the staff is getting situated, trading little stories with one another, figuring out where to sit, and worrying about what they did not get done. In short, they are not giving the supervisor their full attention. It is best to give out general information during this settling in time, things that are not earth shattering if they forget. Joshua told his staff during this part of the meeting that Monday would be a day off from work. If someone forgot that, and worked anyway, it would not be too big of a problem.

Once your staff is settled in, begin the real reason for the meeting, such as "Here are the assignments for the week".

Make sure that at some point in the meeting, you repeat the important information. If it is detailed, make sure that they take notes.

If you are a person who jokes, it is O.K. to do so during a meeting. Make sure that they are jokes that apply to the entire group, and are not private jokes between you and one staff member. If you are not a person who jokes, then do not joke in the meeting.

Make sure that the meeting does not last too long. Anything over an hour is too long for anyone to sit in one place. If you have long meetings, they will lose their effect, and people will start to avoid them.

Analysis: Why Have Meetings?

Supervisors often avoid having meetings because they do not want to take the time or because they are uncertain as to how to run them. Some supervisors pervert the idea of meetings by having frequent, spontaneous meetings: "There will be a meeting at one o'clock to discuss the Smith matter". Others pervert the idea by having long, boring or threatening meetings: "Jim, please tell everyone why your project is over budget".

Meetings are for:

- Giving you a chance to give out all of the current information at one time.
- Providing the time to give out weekly assignments.
- Providing a forum for discussions about problems.

- Giving your group a chance to work together, to strengthen their identity.
- Giving you a chance to show that you are in charge.
- Getting your entire staff thinking about the current work.

Meetings are not for:

- Disciplining one employee.
- Giving out long boring speeches.

Meetings should :

- Be weekly.
- Involve the entire group.
- Be brief, 15 minutes to one hour maximum.
- Be relaxed.
- Be informative.
- Be friendly.
- Be regularly scheduled.
- Be conveniently scheduled for the entire staff.
- Be included in the regular pay of the staff.

How the Three Supervisors Do Meetings

Sensitive supervisors have a difficult time with meetings. Anyone with a powerful personality can easily overwhelm a sensitive supervisor and begin to run the meeting themselves.

You are not in charge of your meeting if:

- Someone else determines that a different room, or seating arrangement should be used.
- Someone else is writing on the board at the front of the room and you are in the rear of the room.
- You are taking notes and your staff is dictating them to you.
- Someone else talks more than you do, and interrupts you.
- Someone else summarizes at the end.

Belligerent supervisors want to run meetings long and spend time on tangents:

Your meeting is too long or not on point if:

- It lasts more than one hour.
- You talk about the main topic for only five minutes at the end.
- The staff seems confused about their assignments at the end.

Regal supervisors use meetings to try to show that they are in charge, and to try to remove any threat from employees who they fear might take over the supervisor position. The regal supervisor must try to remove this worry and concentrate on their employees.

You are not running a good meeting if:

- Your meeting lasts less than 15 minutes.
- Your staff is confused about their assignments.
- Your staff is laughing at you, rather than with you.
- You allow yourself to be interrupted by telephone calls or visitors during the meeting.

- You have assigned discrete tasks which will take less than half an hour to each of your staff members.
- At the end of the meeting your staff has no clear idea of the direction of the company, or the content of the project.

CHAPTER 11....A NEW WAY TO COMMUNICATE: OVERCOMING RESISTANCE

Exasperated supervisors often ask "why can't they just do it the way that I asked them to?" This question is often followed by "Am I the only one who is thinking around here?"

A Story About a Long Instruction

Ralph wanted to have some flower seeds planted. He asked Matilda to plant them. He was going to be gone the next day, so he caught up with her and explained the process to her. First, moisten the soil, then scratch it up, then put small holes in it for the seeds, put the seeds in and cover them over.

Matilda was anxious to do a good job. The next day she got her supplies together and started. She had a little trouble remembering exactly what Ralph had said. She started. First she put small holes in the soil, inserted the seeds and covered them, then she scratched up the soil and last she watered it.

Ralph came back the next day and found all of the seeds on the top of the soil and at one end of the container. He could not believe that Matilda was so stupid.

Analysis: They Can't Remember

Oftentimes, when it seems that an employee is amazingly stupid, it is because they were given a long involved instruction, and they actually cannot remember all of the parts of it. The easy solution to this is to make sure that detailed instructions are written down.

A Story About Bad Habits

Ruth went to college in the 1970's and majored in Natural Resources. Continually increasing her knowledge of the environment was both her college goal and her lifelong goal.

After college, Ruth took up a hobby of refinishing old furniture. She disregarded all warning labels on the cans of chemicals which she was using, often getting a nauseous feeling, and at times burning sensations on her skin where the chemicals were dripped.

In 1990, Ruth and her life-partner combined their professional experiences to begin a hazardous waste remediation business. They often discussed Ruth's hobby in relation to their business, and Ruth admitted that she could use more safety precautions when she refinished things. But Ruth felt that it was really not worth the effort to move her project outside, open a window, or get protective clothing. She just did not want to.

Analysis: They Just Don't Want To

Often, your employees will be just like Ruth. They will be reasonably intelligent. They will actually know the "right" way to do their work. They will just not want to put forth the effort to change their bad habits in a particular area.

A Story About Changing Habits

After about five years of running a hazardous waste remediation business, and five years of constant reminders by her life-partner, Ruth began to change her habits. First, she looked for more protective clothing. Next, she decided that all chemicals which had strong odors should be used out of doors. She scheduled her painting and paint-stripping times for summer months. Last, she decided that with her respect for the environment, she should begin experimenting with environmentally friendly chemicals.

Analysis: You Can Change Habits, But Slowly

Everyone has some bad habits which they do not want to change. You cannot force them to change, but with constant gentle reminders, over a very long time, they will change.

If your employee has one of these "don't want to" problems, it might be more expedient to find someone else to do that particular task.

A Story About An "Impossible Task"

Aaron had a new "significant other". While his old partner did not mind the fact that Aaron spent three nights a week away from home, his new one did. Each Monday morning Aaron would hear the same thing:

"Why do you have to leave? Can't someone else go? Will you be able to come home early this week?"

Aaron got to work and learned that the proposed task for the week would be difficult and might take more than 40 hours of work to accomplish. He began to worry about telling his significant other, and he was a little irritated that he was being asked to work so hard. He told his supervisor:

"I don't think we can get it done this week. We should plan to do half of it and finish up next week."

His supervisor explained that the project needed to be completed on time.

Aaron left for the field site. Upon arrival he telephoned back and proclaimed that he had forgotten to load up some of the tools that he needed. He was told to purchase replacements. Next he called to say that it was too cold outside to do the work. He was told to put on his insulated coveralls and insulated boots. He continued to call back with problems which stopped his work, and at the end of 40 hours of work, he had less than one day of the project accomplished. His supervisor, who was a belligerent supervisor, said:

"You *&$#* well better get that job done. You will not be coming back until you do."

After 80 hours of work on Aaron's part, the project was half accomplished and he finally returned home. He was irritated at his irrational supervisor, and his supervisor was irritated with him.

Analysis: Sometimes "They" Win (in the Short Term)

Sometimes, because of a combination of personal problems, the employee actually sets out with a plan of "I'll show them it can't be done". In these situations it is nearly impossible to convince them otherwise. If you do have them continue on the project, they will resist as strongly as you push. You do need to deal with their attitude and problem, at a later date, but if you want the project to get done, you will have to assign someone else. Sometimes, reassigning them can give them time to reflect and improve their attitude.

CHAPTER 12...A NEW WAY TO COMMUNICATE: EVALUATIONS

A Story About Missy's Evaluation

Missy had worked hard all year. She was especially proud of the fact that she had improved the "bottom line" in her department and it was more profitable than previous years.

It was time for Missy's annual evaluation. Her supervisor had her come into his office and close the door. He had the official company evaluation form on his desk, Missy could see some of the things which were written on it, but she had trouble reading upside down.

Her supervisor said:

"You have done pretty well this year. Your department is doing better than ever. But, I am concerned by the amount of disorder in your department's filing. I see files all over people's desks, I think some valuable information may get lost."

"You deserve a good raise, but this is our company's slow time of year, so I will only be able to give you 50 cents an hour, too bad your evaluation time isn't in the Summer."

Missy was startled by this information. She was incensed that with all of the great work her department had done, they were being evaluated on housekeeping. She was also depressed that she would not be getting a good raise. However, she decided not to contest this evaluation, and she rose to leave. As she was nearly to the door her supervisor said:

"Oh, Missy, you need to work on your people skills."

Missy was not sure what this last comment meant. Were people complaining about her? Did her employees all hate her? She went back to her desk and thought and thought about her evaluation. She started to watch everyone as they came by her, were they smiling? Did it look like they were irritated with her? Missy stewed over her evaluation for the next two weeks. She did very little work. Finally it had receded enough from her memory, that she was able to start to work again.

Analysis: No One Takes Criticism Well

No one likes to sit down and be told what is wrong with them. Corporate evaluations do more to harm the work ethic and productivity of employees than they help.

You can, and should, tell your employees what they are doing wrong, but you should tell them near to the time that you see it. You cannot save up all of the wrongs to be gone over at evaluation time.

If you must do evaluations, always begin them with "How do you think you are doing?" You will find that almost everyone knows exactly where they are doing well and where they are doing poorly. Let them tell you, then you can be the advisor and help them with solutions. If Missy's supervisor had asked her how her department was doing, Missy might have mentioned that she though the housekeeping could be better. Then, instead of an attacker and a defender, there would be two people working together to find a housekeeping solution.

The Three Supervisors and Evaluations

Sensitive supervisors get so nervous about doing evaluations that can effectively send the message to their employee "I am afraid of you". If the sensitive supervisor must do evaluations for their employees, they need to plan what they are going to ask, and concentrate on looking the employee in the eyes, keeping their hands still, and their voice firm.

Belligerent supervisors often use evaluation times to go into long discussions analyzing how the group is working as a whole, and how poorly previous employees worked. They generally have already told the employee if they were displeased with their work. The belligerent supervisor needs to focus on asking the employee questions, and listening carefully to the answers. They also need to watch the time and make sure that they do not run the talk longer than a half hour.

Regal supervisors like to use evaluations to confuse their employees. They are the ones who often end the evaluation with a generic and confusing comment such as "you need to try to get along better with your co-workers", or "the boss really does not like how you park your car". These comments can effectively stop the employee from working well for several weeks. The regal supervisor needs to concentrate on the employee, and focus on helping the employee to do a better job.

CHAPTER 13... A NEW RESPONSIBILITY: FOSTER COOPERATION

A Story About a "Snit-Fest"

Kari went storming into her supervisor's office. She said:

"Janet, you have to help me with Sam, he is always assigning work to my staff. Yesterday he took Alan for the entire day, and now Alan's work is behind. I found Alan this morning and told him that he is not allowed to work on Sam's project."

Janet sighed, and then said:

"Kari, maybe you don't know, but Sam has to get a prototype model out to our client by tomorrow. Since Alan worked on the last model, Sam must have decided that Alan would be the most help."

Kari agreed that this was logical, but she said:

"Why doesn't Sam ever ask me? He just takes my people."

Janet suggested:

"Why don't you ask him that, but wait until tomorrow afternoon, after his prototype has been delivered. In the mean time, can Alan help him out?"

Analysis: Sam Needed to Be Nice

There are two parts to successful work - technical skill and thinking about people. You cannot suspend being kind to others, "just to get the project done". If you do, the project will not get done because the people who you have offended will help to stop it.

Just as your employees will not work well and hard if you have offended them, your co-workers will not help you if you offend them.

Sam needed help so he just took Kari's staff member. Kari responded by forbidding Alan to help Sam. She effectively stopped all work on Sam's project while the problem was sorted out. Their supervisor had to act as a referee in order to get the project started up again.

Getting Along With Others - Foster Cooperation

Robert Fulghum, in his book entitled "All I Really Need to Know I learned in Kindergarten" (*Villard Books, 1988*) observed that those basic rules which were taught to us in kindergarten can carry us through life. To expand upon his idea, the ability to "get along with others" which we need to have in the corporate environment is basically something which is taught to us from a very early age. During our first social interactions, our parents admonished us to not hit or bite other toddlers. In school we learned to get along on the playground and to work in groups to get projects done. Many people seem to feel that when they become adults, these rules no longer apply. But they do. The only way to get work done is to cooperate with most of the other workers on your staff.

The rules for cooperating with others are basically the same as those which we learned as children:

"Childhood Rules"

1. Don't hit.
2. Even if they hit first, don't hit back.
3. Don't steal.
4. Keep your hands and eyes at home.
5. Admit your mistakes and pay for your damages.
6. If you don't like them, then don't play with them.
7. If you don't want to share it, then don't show it to them.
8. When you go out, keep together in a group.
9. Don't be a tattletale.
10. If you can't say anything nice, don't say anything at all.

"Office Rules"

1. Don't hurt others by what you say about them.
2. Even if someone is rude, be nice.
3. Give credit where credit is due.
4. Don't worry about other's work that has no effect on you.
5. If you made the mistake, admit it and fix it.
6. If you don't like them, then avoid working with them.
7. If someone wants to steal your work, hide it.
8. If you are working on a new project, help each other out.
9. Don't be a tattletale.
10. If you can't say anything nice, don't say anything at all.

When the bully on the playground was called to the principal's office, we were all secretly pleased. No one stepped forward to defend the bully. The same thing happens in the office. If you are the "office bully" and show up your peers, take credit due to others and beat out other people for positions and status, you will find yourself standing alone.

If you persist in fighting in the office, just like you did on the playground, you will not get much work accomplished. Cooperate with your peers. Admit your mistakes. Help each other.

SUMMARY OF BOOK TWO

- The sensitive supervisor is afraid to confront anyone.
- The belligerent supervisor wants to yell first and ask questions later.
- The regal supervisor is afraid of losing their job.

A NEW WAY TO BEHAVE

- To be treated like a supervisor, you must act like one.
- You cannot be best friends with your employees.
- You should know how your employees' home life affects their work.
- Always learn from your past experiences.

A NEW WAY TO COMMUNICATE

- Your employee's happiness relates to their sense of control over their job, not their salary.
- You must assign work with a plan for success.
- You must personally monitor the progress of your employees, continually.
- You must train your employees, continually.
- You must have meetings with your employees.
- Traditional evaluations do harm.
- Sometimes people can't remember instructions; write them down.
- Sometimes people don't want to do a task; push them carefully.

FOSTER COOPERATION

- You must help adult co-workers get along with one another.

printed on 20% post consumer recycled paper